I think the series is wonderful and beneficial for tourists to get information before visiting the city.

-Seckin Zumbul, Izmir Turkey

I am a world traveler who has read many trip guides but this one really made a difference for me. I would call it a heartfelt creation of a local guide expert instead of just a guide.

-Susy, Isla Holbox, Mexico

New to the area like me, this is a must have!

-Joe, Bloomington, USA

This is a good series that gets down to it when looking for things to do at your destination without having to read a novel for just a few ideas.

-Rachel, Monterey, USA

Good information to have to plan my trip to this destination.

-Pennie Farrell, Mexico

Great ideas for a port day.

-Mary Martin USA

MOHAMMED AAMIR ALI

Aptly titled, you won't just be a tourist after reading this book. You'll be greater than a tourist!

-Alan Warner, Grand Rapids, USA

Thank you for a fantastic book.

-Don, Philadelphia, USA

Even though I only have three days to spend in San Miguel in an upcoming visit, I will use the author's suggestions to guide some of my time there. An easy read - with chapters named to guide me in directions I want to go.

-Robert Catapano, USA

Great insights from a local perspective! Useful information and a very good value!

-Sarah, USA

This series provides an in-depth experience through the eyes of a local. Reading these series will help you to travel the city in with confidence and it'll make your journey a unique one.

-Andrew Teoh, Ipoh, Malaysia

GREATER THAN A TOURIST – BANGALORE KARNATAKA INDIA

50 Travel Tips from a Local

MOHAMMED AAMIR ALI

MOHAMMED AAMIR ALI

Cover designed by: Ivana Stamenkovic
Cover Image: https://pixabay.com/en/gazebo-canopy-garden-bangalore-332303/

Greater Than a Tourist
Visit our website at www.GreaterThanaTourist.com

Lock Haven, PA
ISBN: 9781980985204

>TOURIST

50 TRAVEL TIPS FROM A LOCAL

MOHAMMED AAMIR ALI

BOOK DESCRIPTION

Are you excited about planning your next trip?

Do you want to try something new?

Would you like some guidance from a local?

If you answered yes to any of these questions, then this Greater Than a Tourist book is for you.

Greater Than a Tourist Bangalore, India edition by Mohammed Aamir Ali offers the inside scoop on Bangalore, located in the southern India. Most travel books tell you how to travel like a tourist. Although there is nothing wrong with that, as part of the Greater Than a Tourist series, this book will give you travel tips from someone who has lived at your next travel destination.

In these pages, you will discover advice that will help you throughout your stay. This book will not tell you exact addresses or store hours but instead will give you excitement and knowledge from a local that you may not find in other smaller print travel books.

Travel like a local. Slow down, stay in one place, and get to know the people and the culture. By the time you finish this book, you will be eager and prepared to travel to your next destination.

MOHAMMED AAMIR ALI

TABLE OF CONTENTS

DEDICATION

This book is dedicated to a dear friend, who loves what I write and motivates me to write more and better myself. This book is also dedicated to love for travel shared by us.

Reaching out, sharing, and caring.
The spring is always around the corner.
Thank you!

MOHAMMED AAMIR ALI

ABOUT THE AUTHOR

Mohammed Aamir Ali has been travelling all over India for various reasons and now lives in Bangalore. Coming from a small town in the state of Karnataka, he had to move to several places in pursuit of education. This resulted in instilling the love for travel in him. More the destination, he loves the journey and the road. His favorite mode of travel is public transport as he gets to learn a plethora of things in a short duration.

He has now decided to settle down in Bangalore where he studied Master of Business Administration. He went on to carve a career for himself in advertising. Having now spent more than 4 year in Bangalore and falling in love with the city, the place has adopted him as one of its own.

One of the things he loves about Bangalore is the never ending places to see in the city and hundreds of places around it that he can visit over a weekend. Weekend come, he takes off on a motorcycle to explore the outskirts, the places not every local knows about.

MOHAMMED AAMIR ALI

HOW TO USE THIS BOOK

The Greater Than a Tourist book series was written by someone who has lived in an area for over three months. The goal of this book is to help travelers either dream or experience different locations by providing opinions from a local. The author has made suggestions based on their own experiences. Please do your own research before traveling to the area in case the suggested places are unavailable.

MOHAMMED AAMIR ALI

FROM THE PUBLISHER

Traveling can be one of the most important parts of a person's life. The anticipation and memories that you have are some of the best. As a publisher of the Greater Than a Tourist book series, as well as the popular 50 Things to Know book series, we strive to help you learn about new places, spark your imagination, and inspire you. Wherever you are and whatever you do I wish you safe, fun, and inspiring travel.

Lisa Rusczyk Ed. D.
CZYK Publishing

MOHAMMED AAMIR ALI

OUR STORY

Traveling is a passion of the "Greater than a Tourist" series creator. Lisa studied abroad in college, and for their honeymoon Lisa and her husband toured Europe. During her travels to Malta, an older man tried to give her some advice based on his own experience living on the island since he was a young boy. She was not sure if she should talk to the stranger but was interested in his advice. When traveling to some places she was wary to talk to locals because she was afraid that they weren't being genuine. Through her travels, Lisa learned how much locals had to share with tourists. Lisa created the "Greater Than a Tourist" book series to help connect people with locals. A topic that locals are very passionate about sharing.

MOHAMMED AAMIR ALI

WELCOME TO
> TOURIST

MOHAMMED AAMIR ALI

INTRODUCTION

*"To see the world, things
dangerous to come to, to see behind
walls, draw closer, to find each
other, and to feel. That is the
purpose of life."*

- James Thurber, The Secret Life of Walter Mitty

Bangalore is a city in located in Karnataka (earlier known as Mysore state) in South India. The city is world renowned due to the presence of several MNCs and its I.T industry. Who can forget the outsourcing industry that got the city into the world's eyes? It is famously called the 'Silicon City of India', 'Concrete Jungle' and is considered to be the I.T capital of the country. Many say that once you stay in Bangalore you can never move back, rightly so, owing to several great things that the city has to offer.

The geographical location of the city is such that it has pleasant weather all round the year. The city has rushed in top speed towards progress but has still managed to preserve its old school charm, thanks to

13

the cultural and traditional practices. Bangalore is a hub of travelers. You can explore the city and then head out to several of the places that are within a few hours' drive. Moreover, Bangalore provides easy access to the whole of south India.

You will be surprised to discover how modernism and tradition have found the harmony in the city. While one part of the city is adorned with high rise structures, the other part has buildings dating back centuries. Welcome to the beautiful city.

1. WHAT'S IN A NAME?

Let us start by getting you familiarized with the toponymy of Bangalore. Bangalore was renamed, more precisely, restored to its original name Bengaluru. Although it is still colloquially referred to as Bangalore, the official documents have done always with the anglicized name and switched to using Bengaluru. The capital city of Karnataka state got its name restores on 1st November, 2014. The name change was proposed by a renowned Kannada writer named U R Anantamurthi way back in 2006. It took the central government eight years to implement the suggestion.

The earliest hint to the name 'Bengaluru' was found in ninth-century. An inscription dating back to 890AD says that the city has a history of more than 1000 years. Exploring the pages of history we come to know that there is an epitaph written in old Kannada at Parvathi Nageshwar temple (Begur) referring a 'Bengaluru war' that happened in 890AD. The district was a part of Ganga Kingdom until 1024 C.E and that time it was called as 'Bengaval-Ooru' meaning the '*City Of Guards*' in old Kannada.

2. THE CITY OF GARDENS

Until the early 21st Century, Bangalore was known for the canopies of trees that lined its busy roads (still visible in some parts of the city). This abundance of greenery earned it the nickname, 'Garden City of India', rightly so due the presence of gardens that sprawl over hundreds of acres!

The popular ones and the ones you MUST not miss are the Cubbon Park and the Lalbagh. The other great place is the JP Park in Yeshwanthpur which consists of four large and beautiful lakes, a lawn that expands for over 25 acres and more than 250 different varieties of flora. Go to this park and sit by one of the lakes. Watch the sky and embark on the beautiful feeling of life. This is the third largest park of Bangalore.

3. THE STATE CAPITAL OF KARNATAKA

Originally known as the Mysore State, the new state was formed on 1st November, 1956 and was renamed as Karnataka. Bangalore was designated to be the state capital as it had been for several centuries for several kingdoms. It houses several historical administrative offices. The most famous one is the Vidhana Soudha, the seat of power where the government administers the state from. This building is known for its architecture. Opposite to Vidhana Soudha is the High Court of Karnataka. The High Court functions out of an iconic red brick building.

4. TRAVEL LIKE A LOCAL

If you want to be greater than a tourist, you have to adapt yourself into the skin of a local. One way to do it is to travel like a local. Bangalore offers a surplus of options when it comes to commuting around the city. Be it cheap busses or expensive taxis, Bangalore offers both in surplus. If you are willing to live the life of a local, head over to one of the hundreds of bus stops near you. Local busses let you travel less than 0.1 dollars, but the catch is, the busses are often crowded and you have to push yourself to find a place to stand in a bus filled to more than its capacity. Don't be surprised if you see a bus so crowded that a few passengers will be hanging outside the door. Bangalore also has a thorough but often crowded local bus network.

The other more popular option is to hail one of the passing auto rickshaws. Be prepared to haggle for the correct fare or insist that they go by meter. More often than not the rickshaws refuse to go to a certain place due to the distance or the traffic. The alternative is to ask to be dropped to the nearest place so that you can catch another rickshaw. The most popular practice of hailing an auto rickshaw is not signaling it with a gesture of hand but by shouting '*AUTO*' at the top of your lungs. You will be spoiled for choice as more than one rickshaw will drop in front of you.

Of course, there is Uber as well and many other similar taxi aggregators like Ola, TaxiForSure, etc. The popularity of these app based taxis has increased manifold due to the convenience. You can book anything from a shared cab (car pool) to a premium cab. A few cab aggregators even let you book an auto rickshaw right from the app at a very competitive price.

5. GRAPE TOURS: THE VINEYARDS OF BANGALORE

Oenophilia. (n) [ee-nuh-fĕh-é-uh] an eternal love or obsession for wine. For wine lovers and connoisseurs, there is nothing more exciting than a short trip to a good winery. So, when it comes to wine tours in Bangalore, this city will offer you several choices. Vineyard tours, making and tasting sessions and grape stomping are what you will find on a wine tour.

Wine lovers flock for these wine tours in Bangalore to taste their favourite blend of wine. A classic wine tour gives you the opportunity to unwind amidst the charming view of the vineyard.

A few vineyards you can find in this city are:
1. Soma Vineyard
2. Grover Vineyard
3. Heritage Winery
4. Nandi Valley Winery

6. STREET FOODS OF BANGALORE

Bangalore is heaven for food lovers. The gorgeous city not just offers a beautiful weather but also offers countless options with binge-worthy street food joints in Bangalore that are scattered all across the city. An Epicure's paradise, Bangalore is just perfect for everything that you would like to try, from midnight eateries to cuisines from all over the country for that delicious quick bite, this city has it all. Head over to the following places around the city for the best street food in the state!

1. V.V. Puram Food Street: Treat yourself to the hot and spicy Masala Dosa and the mouth watering Dal Holige

2. Central Tiffin Room – Malleshwaram: Serving the delicious Butter Masala Dosa for hundreds of patron every hour for over sixty decades, Central Tiffin Room has etched itself a place in the history of Bangalore for its effortless handling of demand and maintaining the consistency of deliciousness.

3. Shivajinagar Eat Street: The name Shivajinagar is synonymous for non vegetarian

delicacies; the streets of Shivajinagar are filled with carts full of meat. Few of the must try items are Kheema samosas, grilled chicken, Idiyappam, sheekh kebabs (chicken, mutton and beef) and the biryanis (chicken and mutton).

4. Johnson Market Chat Street: The chat street is located in the junction of Shivajinagar and Johnson Market. Equally famous as its neighboring eat street, this area serves the need of the vegan patrons as well. All the delicacies served in Shivajinagar are available and in addition must try delicacies here are Suleimani Chai, Harira, Coconut and Fruit Naans and flavored sodas, and of course Phirni (a dessert).

7. FLY HIGH LIKE A KITE

We have all dreamt of flying a plane. In Bangalore you can make that dream come true. With little or no prior experience of flying or a pilot's license, you can enjoy Mircrolight flights which seat up to 2 people.

You can even take charge of the cockpit if you are one of those confident types! Microlight flight last for up to 20 minutes.

8. CITY GONE WILD

Have you ever heard of a wild life reserve in a city? Bannerghatta National Park and zoo is just 10 miles from the city. It provides asylum to a plethora of flora and fauna. The national park is an assortment of various establishments such as Bannergahtta Biological Park, Wildlife Safari, Butterfly Park, Anekal Range forest, Children's Park, museum, etc. The massive sanctuary is spread across 65,127.5 acres and is situated at an elevation of 1245 - 1634m. The area is surrounded by hills. The nature is so abundant here you will be amazed that such a place exists so close to a city that is known as the 'Concrete Jungle'.

Nature lovers and photography enthusiasts are in for a treat the moment they enter the area. Take a safari and spot Tigers in their natural habitat. Not just Tigers, wildlife here include Elephants, Leopards, Jackal, Fox, Wild Boar, Sloth Bear, India Gazelle, Spotted Deer, Porcupine, Asiatic Lion, Monitor Lizard and Cobras. Get caged in a jeep and watch the animals roam free. Don't miss the Butterfly Park. Butterfly Park is made of glass and is home to hundreds of species of Butterflies. Enjoy the feeling of these winged creatures flying around and landing on you while you learn about them at close quarters. The park covers an area of 7.5 acres and has a museum, conservatory and an audiovisual room. The conservatory can house about twenty species of butterflies and has its own artificial ecosystem that provides the perfect conditions for them to thrive and flourish.

Bannerghatta National Park is a unique learning experience for both adults and children alike. In addition to being a natural retreat, the park is also an unlikely destination for a wide variety of adventure sports such as trekking and hiking.

9. TOUCH THE HEAVENLY SKY

Bangalore is not just about high rise corporate structures. There are several places for the trekking enthusiasts. Drive in any direction for a few miles and you will find a place to trek. Tours and guides are available for both day time and night treks. Few of the places for the best experience are listed below.

1. **Kuntibetta**: Situated at a distance of 120 K.Ms from the city, this place offers an exhilarating experience while you try to reach the top. Night treks are most preferred experience due to the mesmerizing view of the Milky Way from the top. Lie down on one of the rocks and enjoy the lost please of star gazing. Make sure you have the list of your wishes ready as you are about to witness several shooting stars! As the sun begins to rise and the mist clears, it is a sight to behold and cherish for the rest of your life. There will be a few groups of trekkers as the sun rise time nears. The moment the sun starts being visible on the horizon, the whole place experiences drop dead silence, the view is too good to be spoiled by engaging in a conversation. The trek level is easy and even a beginner can make it to the top.

2. **Ramnagar Trek**: The town of Ramanagar is located 50 K.Ms from Bangalore. Start early and reach the base point by sunrise and have a

pleasant trek of 1 hour. The peak offers an unforgettable view of several miles around you. On a clear day, you can catch a glimpse of the Bangalore as well. Do not miss the 'Sholay Spot', the place where the cult Indian Western movie *Sholay* was shot. Though the trek is very easy, you should avoid it during summers as the town tends to get too hot.

3. **Nandi Hills**: Perhaps the most famous trekking place, Nandi Hills is 60 K.Ms from the city. This is also the easiest yet the most beautiful trek in the area. You can drive most of the way and trek the remaining part as you explore the fort whose walls go around the entire hill! You will find yourself above the clouds. The Tipu drop point is a famous spot that offers a panoramic view of the surroundings. Beware; the place tends to get very chilly early in the mornings.

4. **Savanadurga**: This is a hill about 60 K.Ms from Bangalore. Situated at the elevation of 1227 meters is one of the largest monoliths in the whole of Asia. A mesmerizing huge rock welcomes you at the end of the Savanadurga

village. A small trek later you arrive at the foot of the hill. A difficult steep climb and hopping from rock to rock, you will find yourself amongst the ruins of the fort which once belonged to Kempegowda, the erstwhile king and founder of the modern Banaglore. It is advised to pack a few snacks as there are no places to eat except for a few coconut vendors.

5. **Avalabetta**: Past the green fields of a town called Chickaballapura are the hillocks that extend beyond the horizon. One of these is a hill that goes by the name Avalabetta. A favorite among weekend bikers as it is just an hour's drive from the city. An easy trek to engage in, this hill offers a sight that is better than in Disney movies. This hill is in the same range as that of Nandi hills but several K.Ms apart making it a whole new experience.

10. TOO FAR FROM THE SEA, BUT STILL WANT TO SCUBA DIVE?

If your itinerary of South India travels include visiting the oceans and wanting to scuba dive you are in for a good time. Travelers want to fit in as many activities as they can in their schedule. If scuba diving is one of those activities and you want to take a few lessons before heading out into the waters, you can easily do so while you in the city itself. The nearest sea to Bangalore is several hours of drive away. You are in luck as the City has several institutes that offer training on scuba diving. It's true what they say; you are never far from anything when you are in Bangalore!

Head over to the following institutes for the best lessons.
1. Dive India: Vittal Mallya Road
2. Planet Scuba: Indiranagar
3. Aquanaut India: Langford Town

11. TAME THAT STALLION

Let your stress gallop away while your hair enjoys the wind. You don't have to venture too far from the city to enjoy Horse rides. The experience of learning horse riding is for both a first timer and a person who has ridden before. You can learn the basics of horse handling, riding, and untacking.

12. THE HIDDEN BANGALORE

Tour, what is perhaps the oldest part of Bangalore, the pete (pronounced pay-tay). Go back to a couple of centuries as your story guide tells you the story of the vanished medieval fort and takes you through the bazaar filled maze of the tiny street markets in the area. The areas like Shivajinagar and KR Market are definitely a worthy visit to see how the Old Bangalore functions. Shop till you drop at these places which offer cheap things to buy.

These areas are mostly market places and you can find anything for retail purchase as well as wholesale shopping at unbelievable places. It is referred to as

Old Bangalore because the town started growing from these places. The market places like Majestic, K.R Market, and Shivajinagar were scattered and once the city started growing, all these were considered as old areas. It is advised to visit these laces escorted by a local guide as the places are a maze and nightmare to navigate.

13. THE UBER LUXURIOUS UB CITY

UB City is a locality in the city which truly displays the luxurious face of Bangalore. The shopping malls, high-end entertainment centers, 5 star restaurants, sky scrapers that can hurt your neck if you want to see the top from the ground; UB City has everything to offer and more! The complex expands over an area of 13 acres, is the biggest luxury complex in Bangalore. It is as if a piece of Europe was transported to this city. UB City has four towers namely, UB Tower (19 Floors), Comet (11 Floors), Canberra (17 Floors) and Concorde (19 Floors).

14. THE ARTSY BANGALORE

If you are a culture and classical art enthusiast, you should head to Karnataka Chitrakala Parishath. It was established in the year 1960 by late M. Arya Murthy and late Prof. M.S Nanjunda Rao. It is a heaven for art lovers. It houses painting from the bygone era of princely India. You will also find several paintings and sculptures from renowned foreign artists. The complex has 18 galleries. 13 of these galleries carry a permanent collection of paintings, sculptures and folk art. The other galleries are rented out for exhibitions of works by artists of repute. If you are here in January, you can treat yourself to beautiful art at the annual *'Chitra Sante'* meaning 'Art Market'. It is organized with the motto of 'Art for All' to promote affordable art for everyone.

Address: No.1, Art Complex, Kumara Krupa Road.

Timings: 10 AM – 6:30 PM (Closed on Sunday)

15. FAN OF MODERN ARTS?

Bangalore has a way of impressing everyone. Head over to the National Gallery of Modern Arts, a museum housing paintings by modern & contemporary Indian artists, plus a cafe & an auditorium. The gallery has an impressive collection of paintings and sculptures from renowned artists. It is also a haven for new artists. See the budding artists before the world does. It was established in the year 2009 and houses paintings from world renowned Indian artists such as Raja Ravi Verma, Jamini Roy, Amrita Sher-Gil, Rabindranath Tagore and others. The building itself is a work of art as the museum is housed in a century-year-old mansion – the former vacation home of the king of Mysore.

Address: #49, Palace Road, Manikyavelu Mansion.

Timings: 10 AM – 5 PM (Closed on Monday)

16. DISCOVER THE WORLD OF LITERATURE

Stephen King aptly declared books to be 'the uniquely portable magic'. Church Street, located adjacent to the M.G Road and Brigade Road (Two of the busiest commercial roads in India) is a quaint little street sprinkled with every kind of shop ranging from eateries in its every nook and cranny, to tattoo parlors, bowling alleys and pubs. But most notably it is a hub for literature lovers. The street is a means to disappear into the magical world. It is famous due to the abundance of book stores raging from iconic British era stores to multi chain stores. It is home to some of the most unique bookstores in the world. The aisles are made from the stacks of thousands of books that make the shopping experience almost like an archeological hunt. Don't be surprised if you stumble upon a limited edition collectible. I can easily spend a week inside a single store. You can buy all the latest releases as well as lost in history classic used books.

Few of the iconic book stores are listed below. Make sure you visit each one of these as each has been a part of Bangalore's history and popularizing the reading habit since ages:

1. Blossom Book Store
2. Sapna Book House
3. The Bookworm
4. Gangaram's Book Bureau
5. Higginbotham's: A store famous as the official book stores for His Highness the Prince of Wales.
6. Select Book Store

17. WANT TO FLY BUT DON'T WANT IT TO BE AN AIRPLANE?

Zoom across the sky is a Para motor. A Para motor takes you up to 4000 ft into the sky. Feel like a bird during this 15 minute joy ride. You will of course be accompanied by an instructor while you get a bird's eye view of the beautiful city.

18. BAKE AWAY YOUR WORRIES

For all those who are culinary enthusiast, Bangalore has several places where you can learn the art of baking. It is great to sit by the roadside café in the romantic streets of Paris, but it is even better when you can have a piece of cake that you baked on your own. It is high time you add this skill to your list.

19. THE AYURVEDIC WAY

India is known for Ayurveda, an age old medical practice of using herbs to cure ailments. Indulge yourself in some Ayurvedic Spas. Let your stress be massaged away into oblivion. Bangalore has hundreds of spas that offer Ayurvedic massages and other treatments.

20. PARASAIL WITH YOUR PARTNER

Are you an adventure junky couple? Then parasailing is something that you and your partner must try! Only thing better than the wind in the hair is when you get a view that you'll never forget! Be assured, life cannot get better than this.

21. MUSIC TO THE EAR

Indiranagar and M.G. Road are the areas that are the hubs for pubs and live music bars. Have a good time with some good live music playing in the background.

These mini concerts are a haven for budding musicians ranging from Indie music scenes to pure metal heads. You might even catch a famous band playing (Coldplay once surprised a pub's patrons in the city by paying a surprise visit and performing.)

22. COME, SEE, CONQUER YOUR BODY

If one thing India is known for more than Ayurveda, it is the Yoga. Attend short crash courses on Yoga and carry this experience back home.

Not everyone gets to heal themselves physically and mentally while they travel and Bangalore certainly offers this option. Give your body a new life by learning Yoga here and practicing back home.

23. A MODERN TEMPLE OF FAITH

Who says temples should be old and ruined to be enjoyed? ISKCON temple is a Hindu place of worship dedicated to Lord Krishna and is as modern as it can be.

ISKCON stands for The International Society for Krishna Consciousness. Interestingly enough, ISKCON was started as a society way back in 1966 in New York.

24. THE COMMERCIAL STREET

The Commercial Street in Shivajinagar is one of the oldest and the busiest business areas of Bangalore. You will find traders selling clothes, jewellery, footwear, and electronics at dirt cheap prices. Tourists, students, and locals throng this street to shop at very low prices. When you get tired of walking around you can hit the street side for some of the most amazing street food joints in the world.

The amazing places for street food are the Shivajinagar square and the Johnson Market which have been discussed earlier in the book.

25. THE ROYAL SUMMER RETREAT

Hidden in the streets of K.R Market is the two storied summer palace of Tipu Sultan, the erstwhile king of Mysore Kingdom. The palace was used for administrative purposes of the Bangalore region and also as a summer retreat for the king. The palace is constructed in Indo-Islamic style and in most parts, made out of wood. The ground floor is now converted into a museum to show case belongings of Tipu Sultan such as his clothes and rockets.

26. THE THEATER SCENES

If you are a fan of theater, head straight to Ranga Shankara. Ranga Shankara is one of the oldest and most notable theaters of Bangalore for indie plays. You can catch a show any day of the year and tickets are very reasonably priced. You can spot several notable theater and literary personalities here.

27. THE CHINNASWAMY CRICKET STADIUM

Cricket is considered to be a religion in India. It is undisputedly the most popular game of the country. Bangalore is blessed with a world class cricket stadium. You can catch matches between regional teams and if your timing is right, you can witness an international match as well. But beware; getting a ticket to the matches is very difficult and you need to act fast.

28. DEATH BY CHOCOLATE

Corner House is a chain of ice cream parlors in South India. All the Corner House ice cream parlors will be in the corner buildings. Death by Chocolate (DBC) is a chocolate ice cream that seems to be straight out of heavens, you should never go back from Bangalore without treating yourself with a DBC. It will be so reach in chocolate that you will need a long time to finish it if you are eating it alone. Forget that diet plan, indulge yourself for once.

29. VISVESVARAYA INDUSTRIAL AND TECHNOLOGICAL MUSEUM

Built on a 43000 sq. ft. area and opened to the public in the year 1962, Visvesvaraya Industrial and Technological Museum is dedicated to the renowned engineer and a pioneer of industrialized India, Sir M. Visveswaraya.

VITM has a Dinosaur Corner with mobile app facility & a 1:1 scale replica of the Wright Brothers' Flyer "Kitty Hawk" along with 'Flyer Simulator' providing an immersive and entertaining experience to the visitor. The 'Science on a Sphere' at VITM, the only one in Asia, is a large visualization system that uses multimedia projections to display animated data on the sphere converting it into an immersive animated globe showing dynamic, animated images of the atmosphere, ocean's and land area of a planet, combined with narration.

VITM has 7 permanent exhibition galleries titled Engine Hall, Fun Science, Electrotechnic, Space –

Emerging Technology in the Service of Mankind, Biotechnological Revolution, BEL Hall of Electronics and Children Science.

Vishvesvaraya Industrial Museum, Bangalore and the Smithsonian Institutions in the U.S are the only places in the world where you can find a full scale replica of the 1903 plane built by Wright Brothers. Each floor of this museum is dedicated to a particular field of science. If you are a fan of technology or you have a kid accompanying you, you must never miss this one.

Address: Near Chinna Swamy Stadium, Kasturba Road.

Timings: 10 AM – 6 PM (Open 7 days a week)

30. DERBY LOVERS REJOICE

Horse lovers rejoice at the Bangalore Turf Club. The Bangalore Race Course is probably the only one on the world where a limited space of barely 85 acres has been so comprehensively utilized to provide facilities such as stabling for over 1000 horses, three training tracks, an equine swimming pool, training schools, walking rings, a veterinary hospital and even an amateur riding school. The Derby is a visual treat- horse racing, spotting celebrities and off the ramp fashionistas.

31. THE HAL AEROSPACE MUSEUM

Bangalore is not the place that will disappoint a fan of aeronautics. The HAL Aerospace museum is the second largest museum in India dedicated to the aeronautics. It was establishes by Hindustan Aeronautics Limited (HAL) and showcases the aeronautical history of India and the achievements of the HAL. You will get to enjoy the realistic fighter jet stimulator a price that is less than a dollar.

There are two major halls, one displaying the photographs that chart the growth of aviation in each decade from 1940 till date and a Hall of Fame that takes the visitors on an exciting journey through the Heritage of Aerospace & Aviation Industry in India. The second Hall highlights the various functions of an Aero Engine by displaying motorized cross sections of various models of Aero Engines. Real Engines such as Garret (for Dornier Aircraft), Adour (for

41

Jaguar Aircraft) and Orpheus (for Kiran Aircraft) can be seen here along with Ejection Seat with Parachute; and Pushpak & Basant Aircraft.

Their most unique exhibit is the ATC Radar parched with L Band surveillance Radar having a range of 200 nautical miles which rotates at speed of 3-4 RPM, with the frequency of 1250-1350 MHZ and Meteorological Radar. In addition, PSLV model & PSLV Heat shield are displayed to give a glimpse of forays made by the country in space technology. Fun fact: India successfully launched a mission to Mars on a budget that was lesser than the cost of making the Sandra Bullock space adventure movie 'Gravity', isn't that something?

Address: Near HAL Police Station, HAL Old Airport Road.

Timings: 9 AM – 5PM (Open 7 days a week)

32. RAMAZAN DELICACIES

If you happen to visit Bangalore during the Islamic holy month of Ramazan you are at luck. Ramazan is the holy month for Muslims during which they fast from dawn till dusk. When they break the fast it is called Iftar. Iftar parties are huge and filled with delicacies you will never get to see for the rest of the year. Visit Frazer Town, BTM Layout and Shivajinagar from 5 P.M to 7 P.M and indulge yourself with mouth watering food.

33. DISCOVER THE FUN OF WALKING

Any place in the world is best discovered when you explore it on foot. You will get to see the real face of the city and enjoy it at your own pace. Several Bangalore locals organize walking tours of the city. You can easily discover these activities on any local events websites.

A few of the walking tour providers are:

Bangalore Walks: You can choose from walks such as the "Green Heritage" walks through Lalbagh or the "Military Heritage" one around Madras Engineering Group and the Ulsoor area, soaking up the city's military history. They also have themed tours, ideal for foreign visitors.

MOHAMMED AAMIR ALI

Oota Walks: Oota Walks, founded by Simi Mathew and Shibaji Ghosh, organises food tours around the city's culinary hotspots, from Basavanagudi to Nagarathpete.

Bengaluru by Foot: Started by city-based architect, Mansoor Ali, this group offers everything from heritage walks to food trails. From the Houses of Malgudi walks (to explore some of the oldest houses here that will remind you of the fictional town, Malgudi) to a walk in Nagarathpete that will take you through the weavers' community there, this one's all about getting to know the city up close. They also organize Ramazan Iftar Walks during the Islamic month of Ramazan.

Nandi Valley Walks: The Nandi Valley Walks conducts informative walking trails in and around the foot of the Nandi area. They include stops such as the Bhoganandishwara Temple, which dates back to the 9th century, and an abandoned British cemetery nearby.

34. LIFE IS A CARTOON

Indian Institute of Cartoonists is a one of a kind society in the country. It is wholly dedicated to the art of cartooning and promoting the same. The institute trains and promotes young cartoonists and has a year round display of humor in a few lines in its premises.

35. THE ESCAPE ARTIST

Breakout is the city's first and one of the very few escape room games centre in India. You can enter alone or as a team of 2 to 5 members and escape like James Bonds from a locked room under an hour. Use your leadership, critical thinking, and problem solving capabilities to get your team out of the room or be locked forever.

36. PEDDLE YOUR WAY INTO FUN

Walking isn't the only way to enjoy Bangalore at a slow pace. Unventured Cycle Trail offers bicycle tours of the city. You can select a package based on

45

your interests, duration, and intensity. You can ride into the areas of art, heritage, and culture and even enjoy the food trails. They also offer tours into the outskirts of the city only if you have a lot of time to spare.

37. THE TOY STORY

Channapatna is a town nestled a few miles away from Bangalore on Mysore route. Channapatna is famous for its handmade wooden toys and many more products from wood. The town survives on this industry and is definitely worth a visit. This town is world famous and the toys made here adorn the shelves of White House of U.S.A itself!

38. LET IT SNOW

Experience the pleasure of playing with the snow in the heart of the city. Snow City is a park covering over 12500 sq. ft. where you can play with snow. There are several other activities like snow rock climbing, snow rafting, snow basketball, etc. It is ideal for all age groups. All the necessary gears will be provided.

39. THE PUPPET SHOW

Puppets have been used in India as a tool for story telling for centuries. But this traditional art is dying slowly. This is where Dhaatu Puppet Theatre comes in. This theatre has worked extensively to preserve and promote the ancient art. Dhaatu puppet festival is an event that cannot be missed. Make sure you pay a visit and witness the ancient art in its full glory.

40. EAT WHILE YOU FLOAT

Lumbini Garden in the Nagarvara Lake is a water amusement park. They offer a ton of water based entertainment activities. It stretches over an area of 1.5 K.Ms. The USP of this water amusement park is the boat shaped floating restaurant named 'Golden Pearl'. Enjoy the local delicacies while you float.

41. THE GREEN POCKET

Located in the central Bangalore is a place called Pocket of Green. It is play space for kids. If you are accompanied by kids this place is a must see. The place offers unique experiences for children like gardening, craft, painting, vegetable picking, etc. all the while educating he kids and encouraging them to embrace the outdoors.

42. GO HANDICRAFT SHOPPING

The Karnataka Government has set up the Cauvery Emporium with the sole purpose of promoting handicraft products and supporting the lives of these artisans. Head over to your nearest Cauvery Emporium and get your hand on the priceless Sandalwood products, Rosewood products, Channapatna toys and much more at a great price.

43. DANCE TO THE CLASSICAL TUNE

The Nruthyaganam Dance Village was set up as a traditional gurukul styled dance academy. You will witness various forms of classical dance form from all across the country and the amazing dancers working to preserve the traditional dance forms. The institute organizes a dance festival to mark the arrival of spring and at this festival you can meet the classical dance celebrities from around the globe.

44. UP, UP, & AWAY

Another midair activity you can indulge in at Bangalore is hot air balloon rides. Give in to the wish of flying away at the Jakkur Aerodrome. There is a powered hand glider to enjoy as well. Both of these activities will allow you to fly up to 4000 ft. in the air. Enjoy the view of the landscape below. The aerodrome is spread across 224 acres of land.

45. GET CLOSE TO THE URBAN WILDLIFE

People for Animal, Bangalore chapter organize camps to introduce you to the urban wildlife. Pay a visit to reconnect with nature. You will be educated in rescuing, helping, providing medical care to injured animals, etc. If you stay long enough, you can even assist in rehabilitating and ultimately releasing the animals into their natural habitat.

46. GET SPOOKED AT A CEMETARY

When a city has so much to offer, how can it not have a haunted place? If you love haunted places and paranormal activities visit the Kalpalli graveyard at night. Several people have reported witnessing paranormal presence in the cemetery and recount spooky tales. This is definitely an offbeat thing one can explore.

47. RUN, STROLL, REST AT THE CUBBON PARK

Located in the heart of the city and surrounded by administrative area is a designated 'lung' of the city; the Cubbon Park. It covers an area of 300 acres. It is a green belt region of the city and is an ideal place for nature lovers and those seeking a calm atmosphere. There are several historical structures & administrative offices in and around this park that deserve a visit. An early morning run or an evening stroll, this place is perfect for both.

48. PICNIC AT LALBAGH

The 17th century ruler of the Kingdom of Mysore, Hyder Ali is said to have liked the cool climate of the city and developed a garden for his beloved sister Lal Bi. The garden he built is today known as the famous Lal Bagh Gardens.

Lalbagh Botanical Gardens, meaning The Red Garden in English, is heaven for flora enthusiasts. The renowned glass house here hosts the world famous flower show on the Indian Republic Day and the Independence Day. It is home to largest collection of tropical plants in India and has a lake. Most parts of the garden are surrounded by different blocks of the beautiful residential layout – Jayanagar. Lalbagh remains open daily from 6.00 a.m. to 7.00 p.m. throughout the year. It has a lot of hustle bustle in the morning when the local throng the place for morning walks, picnics and bird watching.

49. JAMIA MASJID

The largest mosque of Bangalore, the Jamia Masjid is located in K.R. Market. It was constructed in 1940 in Rajasthani style. White marble is used extensively lending it a serene environment. The 5 storied mosque was designed by Rayyaz Asifuddin from Hyderabad and is dedicated to Tipu Sultan.

50. DAY OFF AT A RESORT

You can head over to one of the several resorts in and around the city if you need to take a day off touring and want to relax. The city offers resorts of every kind, ranging from 5 star luxuries to reasonably priced ones. Check in and jump in to the pool and wash away your fatigue.

Head over to the following for the best experience:

- The Windflower Prakruthi
- Royal Orchid Resort
- Ramanashree California Resort
- Chairman's Resort
- Palm Meadows

BONUS BOOK

50 THINGS TO KNOW ABOUT PACKING LIGHT FOR TRAVEL

PACK THE RIGHT WAY EVERY TIME

AUTHOR: MANIDIPA BHATTACHARYYA

MOHAMMED AAMIR ALI

Edited by Melanie Howthorne

INTRODUCTION

He who would travel happily
must travel light.

-Antoine de Saint-Exupéry

Travel takes you to different places from seas and mountains to deserts and much more. In your travels you get to interact with different people and their cultures. You will, however, enjoy the sights and interact positively with these new people even more, if you are travelling light.

When you travel light your mind can be free from worry about your belongings. You do not have to spend precious vacation time waiting for your luggage to arrive after a long flight. There is be no chance of your bags going missing and the best part is that you need not pay a fee for checked baggage.

People who have mastered this art of packing light will root for you to take only one carry-on, wherever you go. However, many people can find it really hard to pack light. More so if you are travelling with children. Differentiating between "must have" and "just in case" items is the starting point. There will be ample shopping avenues at your destination which are just waiting to be explored.

MOHAMMED AAMIR ALI

This book will show you 'packing' in a new 'light' –
pun intended – and help you to embrace light
packing practices for all of your future travels.

Off to packing!

DEDICATION

I dedicate this book to all the travel buffs that I know,
who have given me great insights into the contents of
their backpacks.

ABOUT THE AUTHOR

Manidipa Bhattacharyya is a creative writer and editor, with an education in English literature and Linguistics. After working in the IT industry for seven long years she decided to call it quits and follow her heart instead. Manidipa has been ghost writing, editing, proof reading and doing secondary research services for many story tellers and article writers for about three years. She stays in Kolkata, India with her husband and a busy two year old. In her own time Manidipa enjoys travelling, photography and writing flash fiction.

Manidipa believes in travelling light and never carries anything that she couldn't haul herself on a trip. However, travelling with her child changed the scenario. She seemed to carry the entire world with her for the baby on the first two trips. But good sense prevailed and she is again working her way to becoming a light traveler, this time with a kid.

THE RIGHT TRAVEL GEAR

1. CHOOSE YOUR TRAVEL GEAR CAREFULLY

While selecting your travel gear, pick items that are light weight, durable and most importantly, easy to carry. There are cases with wheels so you can drag them along – these are usually on the heavy side because of the trolley. Alternatively a backpack that you can carry comfortably on your back, or even a duffel bag that you can carry easily by hand or sling across your body are also great options. Whatever you choose, one thing to keep in mind is that the luggage itself should not weigh a ton, this will give you the flexibility to bring along one extra pair of shoes if you so desire.

2. CARRY THE MINIMUM NUMBER OF BAGS

Selecting light weight luggage is not everything. You need to restrict the number of bags you carry as well. One carry-on size bag is ideal for light travel. Most carriers allow one cabin baggage plus one purse, handbag or camera bag as long as it slides under the seat in front. So technically, you can carry two items of luggage without checking them in.

3. PACK ONE EXTRA BAG

Always pack one extra empty bag along with your essential items. This could be a very light weight duffel bag or even a sturdy tote bag which takes up minimal space. In the event that you end up buying a lot of souvenirs, you already have a handy bag to stuff all that into and do not have to spend time hunting for an appropriate bag.

I'm very strict with my packing and have everything in its right place. I never change a rule. I hardly use anything in the hotel room. I wheel my own wardrobe in and that's it.

Charlie Watts

CLOTHES & ACCESSORIES

4. PLAN AHEAD

Figure out in advance what you plan to do on your trip. That will help you to pick that one dress you need for the occasion. If you are going to attend a wedding then you have to carry formal wear. If not, you can ditch the gown for something lighter that will be comfortable during long walks or on the beach.

5. WEAR THAT JACKET

Remember that wearing items will not add extra luggage for your air travel. So wear that bulky jacket that you plan to carry for your trip. This saves space and can also help keep you warm during the chilly flight.

6. MIX AND MATCH

Carry clothes that can be interchangeably used to reinvent your look. Find one top that goes well with a couple of pairs of pants or skirts. Use tops, shirts and jackets wisely along with other accessories like a scarf or a stole to create a new look.

7. CHOOSE YOUR FABRIC WISELY

Stuffing clothes in cramped bags definitely takes its toll which results in wrinkles. It is best to carry wrinkle free, synthetic clothes or merino tops. This will eliminate the need for that small iron you usually bring along.

8. DITCH CLOTHES PACK UNDERWEAR

Pack more underwear and socks. These are the things that will give you a fresh feel even if you do not get a chance to wear fresh clothes. Moreover these are easy to wash and can be dried inside the hotel room itself.

9. CHOOSE DARK OVER LIGHT

While picking your clothes choose dark coloured ones. They are easy to colour coordinate and can last longer before needing a wash. Accidental food spills and dirt from the road are less visible on darker clothes.

10. WEAR YOUR JEANS

Take only one pair of Jeans with you, which you should wear on the flight. Remember to pick a pair that can be worn for sightseeing trips and is equally eloquent for dinner. You can add variety by adding light weight cargoes and chinos.

11. CARRY SMART ACCESSORIES

The right accessory can give you a fresh look even with the same old dress. An intelligent neck-piece, a couple of bright scarves, stoles or a sarong can be

61

used in a number of ways to add variety to your clothing. These light weight beauties can double up as a nursing cover, a light blanket, beach wear, a modesty cover for visiting places of worship, and also makes for an enthralling game of peek-a-boo.

12. LEARN TO FOLD YOUR GARMENTS

Seasoned travellers all swear by rolling their clothes for compact and wrinkle free packing. Bundle packing, where you roll the clothes around a central object as if tying it up, is also a popular method of compact and wrinkle free packing. Stacking folded clothes one on top of another is a big no-no as it makes creases extreme and they are difficult to get rid of without ironing.

13. WASH YOUR DIRTY LAUNDRY

One of the ways to avoid carrying loads of clothes is to wash the clothes you carry. At some places you might get to use the laundry services or a Laundromat but if you are in a pinch, best solution is to wash them yourself. If that is the plan then carrying quick drying clothes is highly recommended, which most often also happen to be the wrinkle free variety.

14. LEAVE THOSE TOWELS BEHIND

Regular towels take up a lot of space, are heavy and take ages to dry out. If you are staying at hotels they will provide you with towels anyway. If you are travelling to a remote place, where the availability of towels look doubtful, carry a light weight travel towel of viscose material to do the job.

15. USE A COMPRESSION BAG

Compression bags are getting lots of recommendation now days from regular travellers. These are useful for saving space in your luggage when you have to pack bulky dresses. While packing for the return trip, get help from the hotel staff to arrange a vacuum cleaner.

FOOTWEAR

16. PUT ON YOUR HIKING BOOTS

If you have plans to go hiking or trekking during your trip, you will need those bulky hiking boots. The best way to carry them is to wear them on flight to save space and luggage weight. You can remove the boots once inside and be comfortable in your socks.

17. PICKING THE RIGHT SHOES

Shoes are often the bulkiest items, along with being the dainty if you are a female. They need care and take up a lot of space in your luggage. It is advisable therefore to pick shoes very carefully. If you plan to do a lot of walking and site seeing, then wearing a pair of comfortable walking shoes are a must. For more formal occasions you can carry durable, light weight flats which will not take up much space.

18. STUFF SHOES

If you happen to pack a pair of shoes, ensure you utilize their hollow insides. Tuck small items like rolled up socks or belts to save space. They will also be easy to find.

TOILETRIES
19. STASHING TOILETRIES

Carry only absolute necessities. Airline rules dictate that for one carry-on bag, liquids and gels must be in 3.4 ounce (100ml) bottles or less, and must be packed in a one quart zip-lock bag. If you are planning to stay in a hotel, the basic things will be provided for you. It's best is to buy the rest from the local market at your destination.

20. TAKE ALONG TAMPONS

Tampons are a hard to find item in a lot of countries. Figure out how many you need and pack accordingly. For longer stays you can buy them online and have them delivered to where you are staying.

21. GET PAMPERED BEFORE YOU TRAVEL

Some avid travellers suggest getting a pedicure and manicure just the day before travelling. This not only gives you a well kept look, you also save the trouble of packing nail polish. Remember, every little bit of weight reduced adds up.

ELECTRONICS
22. LUGGING ALONG ELECTRONICS

Electronics have a large role to play in our lives today. Most of us cannot imagine our lives away from our phones, laptops or tablets. However while travelling, one must consider the amount of weight these electronics add to our luggage. Thankfully smart phones come along with all the essentials tools like a camera, email access, picture editing tools and more. They are smart to the point of eliminating the need to carry multiple gadgets. Choose a smart phone that suits all your requirements and travel with the world in your palms or pocket.

23. REDUCE THE NUMBER OF CHARGERS

If you do travel with multiple electronic devices, you will have to bear the additional burden of carrying all their chargers too. Check if a single charger can be used for multiple devices. You might also consider investing in a pocket charger. These small devices support multiple devices while keeping you charged on the go.

24. TRAVEL FRIENDLY APPS

Along with smart phones come numerous apps, which are immensely helpful in our travels. You name it and you have an app for it at hand – take pictures, sharing with friends and family, torch to light dark roads, maps, checking flight/train times, find hotels and many other things. Use these smart alternatives to traditional items like books to eliminate weight and save space.

I get ideas about what's essential when packing my suitcase.

-Diane von Furstenberg

TRAVELLING WITH KIDS

25. BRING ALONG THE STROLLER

Kids might enjoy walking for a while but they soon tire out and a stroller is the just the right thing for them to rest in while you continue your tour. Strollers also double duty as a luggage carrier and shopping bag holder. Remember to pick a light weight, easy to handle brand of stroller. Better yet, find out in advance if you can rent a stroller at your destination.

26. BRING ONLY ENOUGH DIAPERS FOR YOUR TRIP

Diapers take up a lot of space and add to the weight of your luggage. Therefore it is advisable to carry just enough diapers to last through the trip and a few for afterwards, till you buy fresh stock at your destination. Unless of course you are travelling to a really remote area, in which case you have no choice but to carry the load. Otherwise diapers are something you will find pretty easily.

27. TAKE ONLY A COUPLE OF TOYS

Children are easily attracted by new things in their environment. While travelling they will find numerous 'new' objects to scrutinize and play with. Packing just one favorite toy is enough, or if there is no favorite toy leave out all of them in favor of stories or imaginary games.

28. CARRY KID FRIENDLY SNACKS

Create a small snack counter in your bag to store away quick bites for those sudden hunger pangs. Depending on the child's age this could include chocolates, raisins, dry fruits, granola bars or biscuits. Also keep a bottle of water handy for your little one. These things do not add much weight and can be adjusted in a handbag or knapsack.

29. GAMES TO CARRY

Create some travel specific, imaginary games if you have slightly grown up children, like spot the attractions. Keep a coloring book and colors handy for in-flight or hotel time. Apps on your smart phone can keep the children engaged with cartoons and story books. Older children are often entertained by games available on phones or tablets. This cuts the weight of luggage down while keeping the kids entertained.

30. LET THE KIDS CARRY THEIR LOAD

A good thing is to start early sharing of responsibilities. Let your child pick a bag of his or her choice and pack it themselves. Keep tabs on what they are stuffing in their bags by asking if they will be using that item on the trip. It could start out being just an entertainment bag initially but with growing years they will learn to sort the useful from the superfluous. Children as little as four can maneuver a small trolley suitcase like a pro- their experience in pull along toys credit. If you are worried that you may be pulling it for them, you may want to start with a backpack.

31. DECIDE ON LOCATION FOR CHILDREN TO SLEEP

While on a trip you might not always get a crib at your destination, and carrying one will make life all the more difficult. Instead call ahead to see if there are any cribs or roll out beds for children. You may even put blankets on the floor. Weave them a story about camping and they will gladly sleep without any trouble.

32. GET BABY PRODUCTS DELIVERED AT YOUR DESTINATION

If you are absolutely paranoid about not getting your favourite variety of diaper or brand of baby food, check out online stores like amazon.com for services in your destination city. You can buy things online ahead of your travel and get them delivered to your hotel upon arrival.

33. FEEDING NEEDS OF YOUR INFANTS

If you are travelling with a breastfed infant, you save the trouble of carrying bottles and bottle sanitization kits. For special food, or medications, you may need to call ahead to make sure you have a refrigerator where you are staying.

34. FEEDING NEEDS OF YOUR TODDLER

With the progression from infancy to toddler, their dietary requirements too evolve. You will have to pack some snacks for travelling time. Fresh fruits and vegetables can be purchased at your destination. Most of the cities you travel to in whichever part of the world, will have baby food products and formulas, available at the local drug-store or the supermarket.

35. PICKING CLOTHES FOR YOUR BABY

Contrary to popular belief, babies can do without many changes of clothes. At the most pack 2 outfits per day. Pack mix and match type clothes for your little one as well. Pick things which are comfortable to wear and quick to dry.

36. SELECTING SHOES FOR YOUR BABY

Like outfits, kids can make do with two pairs of comfortable shoes. If you can get some water resistant shoes it will be best. To expedite drying wet shoes, you can stuff newspaper in them then wrap them with newspaper and leave them to dry overnight.

37. KEEP ONE CHANGE OF CLOTHES HANDY

Travelling with kids can be tricky. Keep a change of clothes for the kids and mum handy in your purse or tote bag. This takes a bit of space in your hand luggage but comes extremely handy in case there are any accidents or spills.

38. LEAVE BEHIND BABY ACCESSORIES

Baby accessories like their bed, bath tub, car seat, crib etc. should be left at home. Many hotels provide a crib on request, while car seats can be borrowed from friends or rented. Babies can be given a bath in the hotel sink or even in the adult bath tub with a little bit of water. If you bring a few bath toys, they can be used in the bath, pool, and out of water. They can also be sanitized easily in the sink.

39. CARRY A SMALL LOAD OF PLASTIC BAGS

With children around there are chances of a number of soiled clothes and diapers. These plastic bags help to sort the dirt from the clean inside your big bag. These are very light weight and come in handy to other carry stuff as well at times.

PACK WITH A PURPOSE

40. PACKING FOR BUSINESS TRIPS

One neutral-colored suit should suffice. It can be paired with different shirts, ties and accessories for different occasions. One pair of black suit pants could be worn with a matching jacket for the office or with a snazzy top for dinner.

41. PACKING FOR A CRUISE

Most cruises have formal dinners, and that formal dress usually takes up a lot of space. However you might find a tuxedo to rent. For women, a short black dress with multiple accessory options will do the trick.

42. PACKING FOR A LONG TRIP OVER DIFFERENT CLIMATES

The secret packing mantra for travel over multiple climates is layering. Layering traps air around your body creating insulation against the cold. The same light t-shirt that is comfortable in a warmer climate can be the innermost layer in a colder climate.

REDUCE SOME MORE WEIGHT

43. LEAVE PRECIOUS THINGS AT HOME

Things that you would hate to lose or get damaged leave them at home. Precious jewelry, expensive gadgets or dresses, could be anything. You will not require these on your trip. Leave them at home and spare the load on your mind.

44. SEND SOUVENIRS BY MAIL

If you have spent all your money on purchasing souvenirs, carrying them back in the same bag that you brought along would be difficult. Either pack everything in another bag and check it in the airport or get everything shipped to your home. Use an international carrier for a secure transit, but this could be more expensive than the checking fees at the airport.

45. AVOID CARRYING BOOKS

Books equal to weight. There are many reading apps which you can download on your smart phone or tab. Plus there are gadgets like Kindle and Nook that are thinner and lighter alternatives to your regular book.

CHECK, GET, SET, CHECK AGAIN

46. STRATEGIZE BEFORE PACKING

Create a travel list and prepare all that you think you need to carry along. Keep everything on your bed or floor before packing and then think through once again – do I really need that? Any item that meets this question can be avoided. Remove whatever you don't really need and pack the rest.

47. TEST YOUR LUGGAGE

Once you have fully packed for the trip take a test trip with your luggage. Take your bags and go to town for window shopping for an hour. If you enjoy your hour long trip it is good to go, if not, go home and reduce the load some more. Repeat this test till you hit the right weight.

48. ADD A ROLL OF DUCT TAPE

You might wonder why, when this book has been talking about reducing stuff, we're suddenly asking you to pack something totally unusual. This is because when you have limited supplies, duct tape is immensely helpful for small repairs – a broken bag, leaking zip-lock bag, broken sunglasses, you name it and duct tape can fix it, temporarily.

49. LIST OF ESSENTIAL ITEMS

Even though the emphasis is on packing light, there are things which have to be carried for any trip. Here is our list of essentials:

- Passport/Visa or any other ID

- Any other paper work that might be required on a trip like permits, hotel reservation confirmations etc.

- Medicines – all your prescription medicines and emergency kit, especially if you are travelling with children

- Medical or vaccination records

- Money in foreign currency if travelling to a different country

- Tickets- Email or Message them to your phone

50. MAKE THE MOST OF YOUR TRIP

Wherever you are going, whatever you hope to do we encourage you to embrace it whole-heartedly. Take in the scenery, the culture and above all, enjoy your time away from home.

On a long journey even a straw weighs heavy.

-Spanish Proverb

PACKING AND PLANNING TIPS

A Week before Leaving

- Arrange for someone to take care of pets and water plants

- •Stop mail and newspaper

- Notify Credit Card companies where you are going.

- Change your thermostat settings

- Car inspected, oil is changed, and tires have the correct pressure.

- Passports and id is up to date.

- Pay bills.

- Copy important items and download travel Apps.

- Start collecting small bills for tips

Right Before Leaving

- Clean out refrigerator.

- Empty garbage cans.

- Lock windows.

- Make sure you have the right ID with you.

- Bring cash for tips.

- Remember travel documents.

- Lock door behind you.

- Remember wallet.

- Unplug items in house and pack chargers.

MOHAMMED AAMIR ALI

READ OTHER
GREATER THAN A TOURIST
BOOKS

MOHAMMED AAMIR ALI

> TOURIST

Visit Greater Than a Tourist for Free Travel Tips
http://GreaterThanATourist.com

Sign up for the Greater Than a Tourist Newsletter for discount days, new books, and travel information:
http://eepurl.com/cxspyf

Follow us on Facebook for tips, images, and ideas:
https://www.facebook.com/GreaterThanATourist

Follow us on Pinterest for travel tips and ideas:
http://pinterest.com/GreaterThanATourist

Follow us on Instagram for beautiful travel images:
http://Instagram.com/GreaterThanATourist

MOHAMMED AAMIR ALI

> TOURIST

Please leave your honest review of this book on Amazon and Goodreads. Please send your feedback to GreaterThanaTourist@gmail.com as we continue to improve the series. Thank you. We appreciate your positive and constructive feedback. Thank you.

MOHAMMED AAMIR ALI

NOTES

39058738R00059

Printed in Poland
by Amazon Fulfillment
Poland Sp. z o.o., Wrocław